Allah
has
Power over
Everything
اللهُ قَادِرٌ عَلَى كُلِّ شَيْء
Green Fig
Proud Muslim Kids
DESIGN & ART BY
Guzel Murtazina

Publisher: Green Fig
Pennsylvania, USA
gogreenfig.com
info@gogreenfig.com
Allah has Power over Everything
ISBN: 978-1-953836-94-6

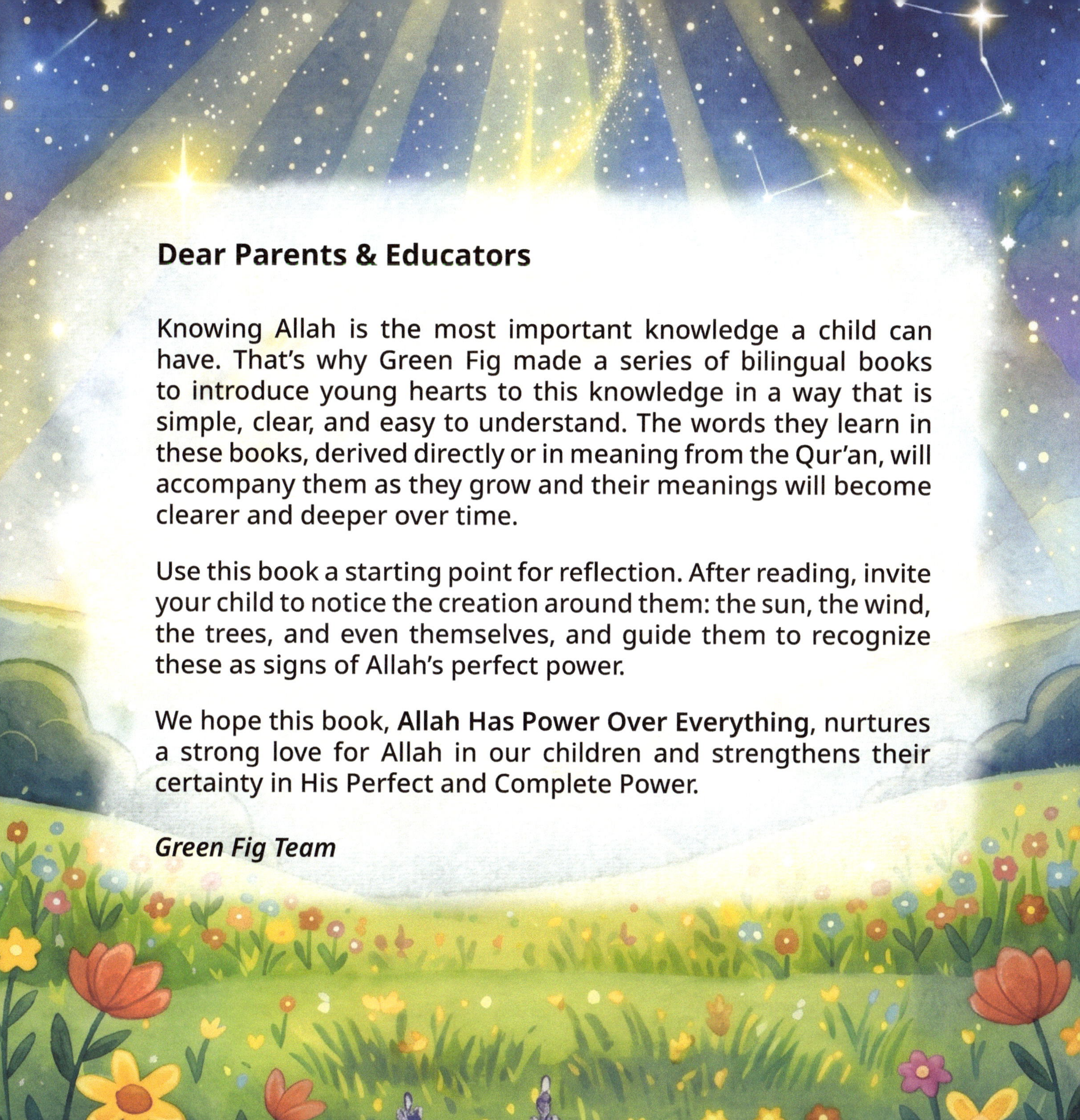

Dear Parents & Educators

Knowing Allah is the most important knowledge a child can have. That's why Green Fig made a series of bilingual books to introduce young hearts to this knowledge in a way that is simple, clear, and easy to understand. The words they learn in these books, derived directly or in meaning from the Qur'an, will accompany them as they grow and their meanings will become clearer and deeper over time.

Use this book a starting point for reflection. After reading, invite your child to notice the creation around them: the sun, the wind, the trees, and even themselves, and guide them to recognize these as signs of Allah's perfect power.

We hope this book, **Allah Has Power Over Everything**, nurtures a strong love for Allah in our children and strengthens their certainty in His Perfect and Complete Power.

Green Fig Team

Allah has power over everything.

اللهُ عَلَى كُلِّ شَيْءٍ قَدِيرٌ.

Nothing is hard for Allah.
اللهُ لَا يُعْجِزُهُ شَيْءٌ.

Allah protects me.
اللهُ يَحْفَظُنِي.

And when I am sick,
He heals me.
إِذَا مَرِضْتُ فَهُوَ يَشْفِينِ.

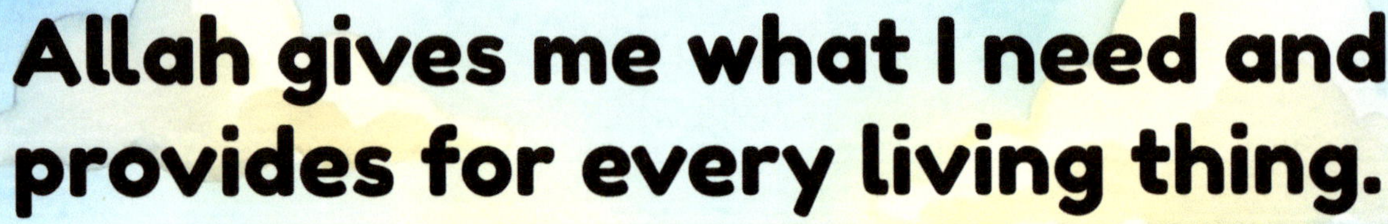

Allah gives me what I need and provides for every living thing.

اللهُ يَرْزُقُنِي وَيُوصِلُ الرِّزْقَ إِلَى كُلِّ مَخْلُوقٍ.

Allah sends down rain from the sky,
اللهُ يُنْزِلُ الْمَطَرَ مِنَ السَّمَاءِ،

and makes a big tree
grow from a tiny seed.
وَيُنْبِتُ الشَّجَرَةَ الْكَبِيرَةَ مِنَ الْحَبَّةِ الصَّغِيرَةِ.

**Allah raised the sky
above us like a roof,**

اللّٰهُ رَفَعَ السَّمَاءَ فَوْقَنَا كَالسَّقْفِ،

and spread the earth beneath
us like a cradle.

وَجَعَلَ الْأَرْضَ تَحْتَنَا كَالْمَهْدِ .

Allah made the sun a bright, shining lamp.

اللهُ جَعَلَ الشَّمْسَ سِرَاجًا وَهَّاجًا.

Allah made the sun rise from the east and set in the west.

اللهُ جَعَلَ الشَّمسَ تَطْلُعُ مِنَ الشَّرقِ وَتَغْرُبُ مِنَ الْغَرْبِ .

Allah gives life and brings death.

اللهُ يُحْيِي وَيُمِيتُ.

Allah makes the dead alive again on the Day of Judgment.

اللهُ يَبْعَثُ الْمَوْتَى يَوْمَ الدِّينِ.

I love Allah who has power
over everything.

أُحِبُّ اللهَ الْقَادِرَ عَلَى كُلِّ شَيْءٍ.

قال الله تعالى:
﴿ إِنَّ اللَّهَ عَلَىٰ كُلِّ شَيْءٍ قَدِيرٌ ﴾
سورة البقرة: ﴿١٠٩﴾